by Robb Armstrong

**Andrews McMeel
Publishing**

Kansas City

VNYS PN 6728 .J86
A75 1997 c.1

CL401

Jump Start is distributed internationally by United Feature Syndicate, Inc.

Jump Start copyright © 1997 by United Feature Syndicate, Inc. All rights reserved. Printed in the United States of America. No part of this book may be used or reproduced in any manner whatsoever without written permission except in the case of reprints in the context of reviews. For information, write Andrews McMeel Publishing, an Andrews McMeel Universal company, 4520 Main Street, Kansas City, Missouri 64111.

www.andrewsmcmeel.com

ISBN: 0-8362-3661-0

Library of Congress Catalog Card Number: 97-71628

Jump Start may be viewed on the Internet at:
www.unitedmedia.com

──────── **ATTENTION: SCHOOLS AND BUSINESSES** ────────

Andrews McMeel books are available at quantity discounts with bulk purchase for educational, business, or sales promotional use. For information, please write to: Special Sales Department, Andrews McMeel Publishing, 4520 Main Street, Kansas City, Missouri 64111.

For Sherry my bride.
Thank you for giving me the love I've needed
to create this work.

JUMP START BY ROBB ARMSTRONG

WELL, WE'VE GONE THROUGH EIGHTEEN BOOKS OF BABY NAMES, AND WE'VE CONSIDERED EVERY NAME IN BOTH OUR FAMILY TREES...

AND WE'VE FINALLY COME TO A DECISION WE BOTH AGREE ON!

NO NAME IS GOOD ENOUGH FOR OUR BABY!

HERE SHE IS! LITTLE BABY GIRL COBB!

LOOK, JOE! HER EYES ARE OPEN!

WOW!

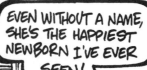

LOOK AT ALL THAT HAIR!

YOU GUYS STILL HAVEN'T DECIDED ON A NAME, HUH?

NO. WE'VE BEEN UP HALF THE NIGHT!

EVEN WITHOUT A NAME, SHE'S THE HAPPIEST NEWBORN I'VE EVER SEEN!

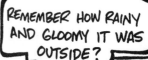

REMEMBER HOW RAINY AND GLOOMY IT WAS OUTSIDE?

YEAH?

AS SOON AS YOUR BABY CAME INTO OUR NURSERY, THE SKY BECAME ALL BRIGHT AND SUNNY!

AND IT'S BEEN SUNNY EVER SINCE!

SUNNY!

6

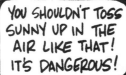

12

JOE AND MARCY, YOU TWO MAY EAT WHEN I'M DONE EATING.

UNLESS, OF COURSE, I'M IN THE MOOD TO SCURRY AROUND ON THE FLOOR LIKE A MANIAC.

YOU EVER WONDER WHO'S IN CHARGE AROUND HERE, MARCY?

NOT FOR A MINUTE, JOE.

GLUG GLUG GLUG

HEY, McELROY, YA GOT SOME MILK ON YOUR SHOULDER.

THANKS, COBB. ...IS THAT CREAMED PEAS ON YOUR COLLAR?

IT'S CALLED THE "NEW DADDY SALUTE."

MY NAME IS DADDY AND HER NAME IS MOMMY!

everybody else calls you joe and marcy!

you two don't even know your own names!

IT SOUNDED LIKE SHE JUST SAID "JOE AND MARCY."

IMPOSSIBLE! SHE DOESN'T KNOW OUR NAMES.

LOOK AT THAT. IT'S HOOTIE AND THE BLOWFISH.

HEH HEH HEH

IS THAT SUPPOSED TO BE FUNNY, CRUNCHY?

IT'S A RACIAL THING, HUH?

ONE BLACK DUDE HANGING AROUND WITH THREE WHITE DUDES IS HUMOROUS TO YOU.

SO YOU AUTOMATICALLY LABEL THEM "HOOTIE AND THE BLOWFISH."

I'M NOT LAUGHING. I'M OFFENDED!

GEEZ. SORRY, JOE. I DIDN'T MEAN ANYTHING BY IT.

YOU GUYS MISSED IT! HOOTIE AND THE BLOWFISH JUST SIGNED A BUNCH OF AUTOGRAPHS HERE AT THE PRECINCT!

21

LOOK WHAT MOM FOUND IN HER ATTIC.

YOUR OLD DR. SEUSS BOOKS!

WOW! "HOP ON POP" "ONE FISH, TWO FISH" "THE CAT IN THE HAT"!

AND ALL OF THEM ARE IN MINT CONDITION!

I'LL BET THESE ARE WORTH A **LOT** OF MONEY, JOE!

AM I **THAT** OLD, MARCY?

HEEHEH HEH HEH HA HA HA HA HA FLIP FLIP

GIGGLE GIGGLE GIGGLE

MY OLD DR. SEUSS BOOKS ARE HILARIOUS!

I THINK SUNNY WAS KIND OF EXPECTING YOU TO READ THEM OUT LOUD.

SUNNY, THESE ARE DADDY'S DR. SEUSS BOOKS...

GRANDMOM AND POP-POP USED TO READ ME THESE WHEN I WAS YOUR AGE.

THEY'VE BEEN PRESERVED IN A BOX FOR YEARS! NOW I CAN GIVE THEM TO YOU!

RIP RIP RIP RIP

WOW! TALK ABOUT A BIZARRE DREAM!

WHAT HAPPENED?

I DREAMED THAT THIS APARTMENT BUILDING WAS BULLDOZED WITH ALL OF US STILL IN IT!

IT'S AN OMEN, JOE! WE HAVE TO BUY A HOUSE!

I HAD THE SAME WEIRD DREAM, BUT WE FLED TO SAFETY IN A NEW ROAD RANGER!

THESE ARE THE CLOTHES AND TOYS THAT SUNNY HAS OUTGROWN...

SINCE THERE'S NO CLOSET SPACE LEFT IN OUR APARTMENT, I'M GOING TO HAVE TO PUT THIS STUFF IN OUR CLOSET AND HIDE OUR WINTER CLOTHES IN THE PARK.

MARCY STILL PUTTING PRESSURE ON YOU TO BUY A HOUSE, HUH?

SHE'S LESS SUBTLE THESE DAYS.

I STUMBLED ACROSS A VERY NICE BROWNSTONE THIS AFTERNOON.

IT'S RIGHT NEAR YOUR PRECINCT, TOO. NEWLY RENOVATED, IN OUR PRICE RANGE.

HOW COME YOU DON'T SOUND VERY EXCITED ABOUT IT?

I DON'T WANT TO BE LET DOWN IF YOU DON'T LIKE IT!

28

JumpStart BY ROBB ARMSTRONG

LET'S AGREE NOT TO BRAG ABOUT SUNNY TONIGHT...

AGREED. NOBODY WANTS TO BE BORED BY THAT STUFF AT A PARTY

THAT'S WHAT THE WORKDAY IS FOR!

WE DID IT, JOE! WE WENT A WHOLE EVENING WITHOUT DWELLING ON SUNNY

HOW ABOUT THAT!

29

JUMP START BY ROBB ARMSTRONG

DID YOU HEAR THAT THE NBA IS GOING TO HAVE A WOMEN'S LEAGUE NEXT YEAR?

I DON'T WANT TO SEE PROFESSIONAL BALL PLAYERS WEARIN' HIGH HEELS, NAIL POLISH AND LIP GLOSS!

THEN I SUGGEST YOU STEER CLEAR OF THE MEN'S LEAGUE AS WELL!

I CAN'T WAIT TO SEE WOMEN IN THE NBA!

NOT ME! I'M AGAINST IT!

WHY?

BECAUSE BASKETBALL IS SUPPOSED TO BE A MAN'S GAME!

WHAT'S NEXT? FEMALE FOOTBALL?

WELL, I'VE SEEN THE WOMEN'S OLYMPIC TEAM IN ACTION... THEY'RE AWESOME!

I'VE SEEN THEM, TOO! IT'S MORE EXCITING THAN WATCHIN' THE GUYS!

THIS NEW LEAGUE WON'T SURVIVE.

TRUST ME.

WE MEN ARE THE BORN ATHLETES!

did you hear the news? sunny hit gavin in the head with the cookie monster puppet!

she did?

gavin started it by putting green jell-o in her hair.

no way!

both of them ended up getting a 2-minute "time out."

oh no!

gavin has stolen my girlfriend!

i think gavin is wonderful!

what?

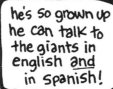

he's so grown up he can talk to the giants in english and in spanish!

plus, he's tall enough to reach the puppets on the top shelf! isn't that amazing?

don't be too impressed. he still poops in his pants just like the rest of us!

looks like gavin has stolen your girlfriend, dexter.

gavin thinks he's going to get away with this, but he won't.

you think you can win sunny back?

of course! after all, what's that guy got that i haven't got?

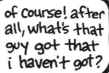

for one thing, his shoes are on the right feet.

39

JUMPSTART

BY ROBB ARMSTRONG

LET'S SEE... WHICH BOOK SHALL WE READ? DR. SEUSS? SESAME STREET? OR MAYBE MICKEY MOUSE...

oh, i don't know

whichever is easiest for you.

?

GREEN EGGS AND HAM BY DR. SE...

wha dat?

I AM SA...

hoo hee?

YOU MEAN THIS GUY?

hoohee daddly?

HE MUST BE A CAT. LIKE THE CAT IN THE HAT.. SORT OF.

not a catinat!

WELL, YOU'RE RIGHT, SUNNY. IT'S NOT THE CAT IN THE HAT. IT'S ..UM... A DOG.

IT'S THE DOG IN THE HAT!

my daddy is having difficulty reading.

41

JUMP START

By Robb Armstrong

ISN'T IT AMAZING?

IT'S ALMOST AS IF THEY UNDERSTAND EACH OTHER!

it's almost as if they understand each other!

i've got a huge crush on sunny.

who's sunny? is she new?

yeah. she's the one with the runny nose and the yogurt all over her shirt.

Say! she is cute!

i spend all my time trying to figure out how to steal sunny away from gavin.

you can't compete with gavin!

gavin's three years old! he can do things! he can reach things, and he can say things!

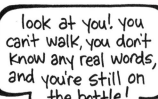

look at you! you can't walk, you don't know any real words, and you're still on the bottle!

i know how to blow spit bubbles.

does sunny know that?!

i've been waiting for just the right moment.

44

45

46

50

53

54

56

JumpStart
by Robb Armstrong

AND NOW... THE MOMENT YOU'VE ALL BEEN WAITING FOR...

LADIES AND GENTLEMEN, BACK BY POPULAR DEMAND...

"SUNNY AND THE SCREAMING INFANTS"!!

WHAT DID YOU THINK OF THE SERMON TODAY?

WHAT SERMON? ALL I COULD HEAR WAS SUNNY AND THE SCREAMING INFANTS!

thank you. thank you very much.

JUMPSTART BY ROBB ARMSTRONG

HOW DID YOU PLAN THAT WHOLE PARTY RIGHT UNDER MY NOSE?

HOW DO YOU KNOW IT WAS MY IDEA?

YOU GOT STUCK CLEANING UP BY YOURSELF!

IT WAS SO NICE OF YOU NURSES TO THROW ME A SURPRISE PARTY!

IT WAS OUR PLEASURE!

MY FAMILY ALWAYS FORGETS MY BIRTHDAY...

HOW SAD.

IT'S OK! I STILL HAVE LOTS OF FRIENDS!

THERE'S ONE NICE YOUNG POLICE OFFICER WHO ALWAYS STOPS BY MY HOUSE TO VISIT ME...

SOMETIMES HE EVEN BRINGS ME FOOD.

HMM... WHAT'S THIS GUY'S NAME?

HIS NAME IS JOE. OFFICER JOE COBB.

THAT'S UNBELIEVABLE! WHAT A SMALL WORLD!

YOU KNOW HIM, HUH?

DOES HE BRING YOU FOOD, TOO?

61

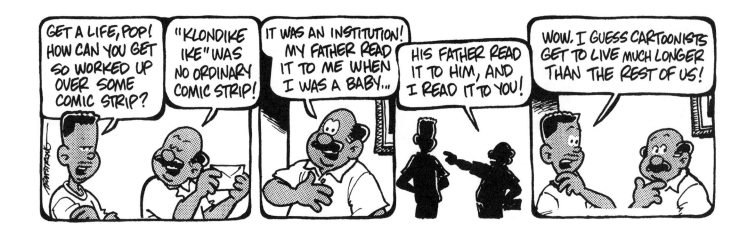

MUST YOU CARRY ON A LONG CONVERSATION WITH EVERY TOLL-TAKER?

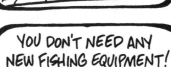
YOU'RE HOLDING UP TRAFFIC!

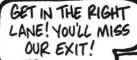
GET IN THE RIGHT LANE! YOU'LL MISS OUR EXIT!

CAN'T YOU FIND A PARKING SPOT CLOSER TO THE MALL?

YOU DON'T NEED ANY NEW FISHING EQUIPMENT!

DON'T TELL ME YOU'RE BUYING HOUSE PAINT!

BE PATIENT, POP! THIS IS THE LAST PAIR I'M TRYING ON!

SLOW DOWN! STATE TROOPERS ARE OUT HERE!

IT WAS NICE SPENDING TIME WITH YOU TODAY, SON.

YEAH. JUST US GUYS!

WITHOUT THE WIVES AROUND TO NAG US.

JUMP START

BY ROBB ARMSTRONG

THEY'RE GOING TO LUNCH!

THE COAST IS CLEAR!

CUTE BABY PICTURES.

THOSE PICTURES ARE OLD.

LOOK AT THESE NEW PICTURES OF SUNNY!

SHE'S WALKING!

AND SHE KNOWS ALL THESE ANIMALS!

COW
DUCK
SHEEP
PIG
HORSE

SHE'S TALKING UP A STORM, TOO!

HA HA HA

SHE'S INVENTED HER OWN LANGUAGE!

YOU HAVE A KID?

UM...YEAH. SHE'S ABOUT SUNNY'S AGE.

BUT NOT AS ADVANCED, RIGHT?

YIKES! HERE COME THE REAL JOE AND MARCY!

LET'S BREAK CAMP!

WHO PUT UP ALL THESE PICTURES OF SUNNY?

OH, NO! OUR EVIL BRAGGING TWINS MUST HAVE BEEN HERE!

73

JUMPSTART

BY ROBB ARMSTRONG

SUNNY'S GOOD STUFF

FRAGILE

JUNK WE SHOULDN'T HAVE PACKED IN THE FIRST PLACE

DON'T EVEN BOTHER HANGING THAT IN THE CLOSET. IT GOES IN THE JUNK BOX.

WHAT A COINCIDENCE.

EVERYTHING IN THE JUNK BOX USED TO BELONG TO ME!

WHY DID WE BRING SO MUCH USELESS GARBAGE WITH US TO OUR NEW HOUSE?

YOU FOUND MY TENNIS RACKET!

DON'T SOUND SO EXCITED. IT'S GOING RIGHT IN THE JUNK BOX.

NOTHING WRONG WITH THIS RACKET.

WOOSH

EXCEPT THAT YOU HAVEN'T USED IT IN FIVE YEARS.

AND THIS WHOLE BOX OF CLOTHES IS OUT OF STYLE! YOU'RE NOT GOING TO WEAR ANY OF THIS STUFF.

IT'S THE PERFECT TIME OF YEAR TO GIVE A BUNCH OF CLOTHES AND STUFF TO THE HOMELESS.

THAT'S A GOOD IDEA, MARCY. NOW YOU'RE THINKIN'!

YOU EXPECT ME TO WEAR THAT? IT'S OUT OF STYLE!

JUMPSTART

Starring JOE & MARCY

"waaeooaa gabboa lppptt!"

"makes you feel old, doesn't it?"

"i think i want to be a baby again."

"what makes you say that, sunny?"

"look at me! i'm sucking my thumb..."

"obviously, i miss my baby bottle!"

"hmph!"

"i think i'm regressing too! i used to love to watch "Bernie the Dinosaur" for example..."

"now, suddenly he terrifies me."

"life was simpler then. no pressures. the giants waited on us hand and foot."

"those were the good ol' days..."

Panel 1: IT'S NOT BAD ENOUGH THAT TWENTY BOXES FLEW OFF THE BACK OF YOUR PICKUP TRUCK!

Panel 2: AND WHAT ROTTEN LUCK FOR A STATE TROOPER TO PLOW HEADLONG INTO A BOX FULL OF HOUSE PAINT!

Panel 3: NOW LOOK AT THIS TICKET! FOUR HUNDRED DOLLARS IN FINES!

Panel 4: MERRY CHRISTMAS!

Panel 5: EXCUSE ME. WHICH ONE OF YOU DO I SUE FOR NEGLIGENCE?

Panel 6: JOE, SANTA CLAUS IS GOING TO SUE US!

Panel 7: YOU HAVE GOT TO BE KIDDING.

Panel 8: I SWERVED TO AVOID THE BOXES YOU GUYS DUMPED ON THE HIGHWAY...

Panel 9: AND MY BMW SLID INTO THE GUARDRAIL, DAMAGING MY CARGO OF TOYS.

Panel 10: I CAN'T BELIEVE SANTA IS REALLY TRYING TO SUE US!

Panel 11: I CAN'T BELIEVE SANTA DRIVES A BMW!

Panel 12: YES! THE SAME ONE 007 DRIVES IN "GOLDENEYE."

Panel 13: HOW AM I GOING TO EXPLAIN THIS MESS TO YOUR WIFE?

Panel 14: SIMPLE! YOU'LL TELL MARCY THE TRUTH:

Panel 15: WE SPILLED OUR MOST TREASURED POSSESSIONS ON THE HIGHWAY.. A STATE TROOPER THEN PLOWED INTO EVERYTHING AND WROTE US A $400 TICKET...

Panel 16: WE CAUSED A FEW MINOR ACCIDENTS, ONE INVOLVING SANTA CLAUS.

Panel 17: NOW SANTA'S GOING TO SUE THE PANTS OFF US.

Panel 18: WE'VE GOT TO COME UP WITH SOMETHING BETTER THAN THE TRUTH.

84

JUMPSTART Starring JOE & MARCY

JOE, LET ME SHOW YOU THIS BANK STATEMENT.

NOT RIGHT NOW, MARCY...

WE DON'T WANT TO TRAUMATIZE SUNNY.

HOW DOES THE BANK COME UP WITH THESE ABSURD FEES?

LOOK AT THESE TWO CHARGES FOR EXAMPLE...

ROBB ARMSTRONG

"SERVICE FEE" AND "MAINTENANCE FEE" SOUND LIKE THE SAME THING TO ME!

NOT TO ME...

I'M SURE THERE'S A BIG DIFFERENCE BETWEEN THE TWO.

BANKING IS WAY TOO COMPLICATED FOR THE AVERAGE PERSON TO UNDERSTAND.

THEY'RE COUNTING ON THAT ATTITUDE, JOE!

THEY DON'T JUST MAKE THIS STUFF UP, MARCY!

OOH! LET'S START CHARGING A "HUMAN CONTACT FEE."

THAT'S THE BEST IDEA SINCE THE OLD "ATM FEE"!

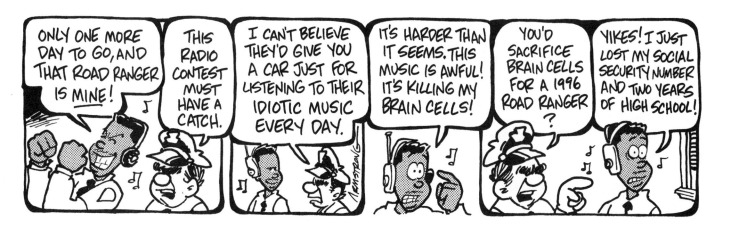

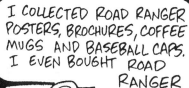

AMAZING! I WANTED A ROAD RANGER MORE THAN ANYTHING IN THE WORLD...

I COLLECTED ROAD RANGER POSTERS, BROCHURES, COFFEE MUGS AND BASEBALL CAPS. I EVEN BOUGHT ROAD RANGER FLOOR MATS!

NOW I FINALLY HAVE THE ACTUAL CAR. I OWN THE ROAD RANGER!

WHY IS WANTING SO MUCH MORE EXCITING THAN HAVING?

SUNNY, YOU'RE BEING TOO BOSSY!

YEAH! THAT'S RIGHT!

I'M THE MOMMY AROUND HERE! HE'S THE DADDY! YOU'RE THE BABY!

WE'RE IN CHARGE, SUNNY! WE MAKE UP THE RULES, GOT IT? WE'RE THE BOSS!

THINK SHE'S BUYING IT?

HECK, I'M NOT EVEN BUYING IT.

HOW COME YOU DON'T LISTEN WHEN I'M TALKING TO YOU?

OH, PLEASE! LOOK WHO'S TALKING!

THIS IS TYPICAL.

YOU GUYS ARE IN A "MARRIAGE" OF SORTS. YOU TAKE EACH OTHER FOR GRANTED.

YOU SHOULD PRACTICE RESPONDING MORE. A RELATIONSHIP NEEDS "GIVE AND TAKES"

WHO ASKED YOU?

ALSO TYPICAL — IGNORING THE THERAPIST.

JUMP START

I WANT TO THANK YOU AGAIN FOR TRUSTING ME WITH THIS BABY-SITTING JOB, MRS. COBB...

YOU DESERVE IT, YVETTE...YOU'RE VERY QUALIFIED!

PLUS, YOU SCORED THE HIGHEST ON MARCY'S EXAM!

YVETTE, HERE'S THE NUMBER TO THE RESTAURANT...

GREAT! HAVE FUN!

OH, AND HERE'S THE CAR PHONE AND MY PAGER, JUST IN CASE.

HERE'S MY PARENTS' NUMBER AND SUNNY'S PEDIATRICIAN'S.

HERE IS THE AMBULANCE NUMBER, JOE'S PARTNER'S HOME PHONE NUMBER, AND THE POISON HOTLINE.

WE KEEP THE FIRE EXTINGUISHER UNDER HERE IF YOU NEED IT.

ON THE INSIDE OF THIS PANTRY DOOR ARE INSTRUCTIONS ON HOW TO PERFORM THE HEIMLICH MANEUVER.

OK.

NOW RELAX AND ENJOY YOURSELF TO SOME EXTENT.

OH...YOU DO KNOW HOW TO LIGHT RESCUE FLARES, DON'T YOU?

Panel 1: YOU'RE NOT COMING TO THE CLASS REUNION? WHY NOT?

Panel 2: BECAUSE YOU DON'T FEEL THAT YOU'VE "ARRIVED" YET? WHAT KIND OF NONSENSE IS THAT?

Panel 3: NOBODY IS GOING TO CLASSIFY YOU THAT WAY! THAT'S ABSURD!

I WISH I COULD CHANGE YOUR MIND.

Panel 4: WHO WAS THAT ON THE PHONE?

SOME LOSER FROM HIGH SCHOOL.

Panel 5: BOY, BEING IN THIS OLD GYMNASIUM AGAIN SURE BRINGS BACK MEMORIES!

Panel 6: I SHOT A BUZZER-BEATER FROM SIXTY FEET TO WIN THE CITY FINALS IN THIS VERY GYM...

Panel 7: I SET A SCHOOL RECORD HERE FOR FOUL SHOTS! I WON MVP TWO TIMES IN THIS GYM.

Panel 8: YOUR MEMORY HAS GOTTEN QUITE VIVID AT YOUR 35TH REUNION, FRANK.

IT'LL IMPROVE EVEN MORE AT MY 50TH!

Panel 9: LOOK OVER THERE. THAT'S HELEN BRAXTON. I TOLD YOU ABOUT HER.

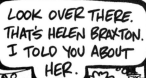

Panel 10: SHE AND I USED TO GO TOGETHER, BUT WE HAD A NASTY BREAKUP.

YEAH, I KNOW THAT NAME.

Panel 11: WE WERE VERY IMMATURE BACK THEN. THAT'S WHY WE SPLIT UP.

Panel 12: SHE'S COMING THIS WAY! QUICK! KISS ME AND MAKE HER JEALOUS!

JUMP START

mickey and his friends sure get a bad attitude at night!

SUNNY! IS THAT YOU?

i'm busted!

SWEETIE, PLEASE SLEEP IN YOUR OWN ROOM TONIGHT!

caught at the border by daddy...

smuggled to safety by mommy!

JUMPSTART

YOUR FOLKS HAVE BEEN SO HELPFUL SINCE WE MOVED INTO THE NEW HOUSE.

YEP. THEY SEEM TO BE HERE CONSTANTLY!

I WONDER IF OUR OLD APARTMENT IS STILL AVAILABLE.

HEY, MOM AND POP...QUIT WORKING FOR A MINUTE. WE HAVE SOMETHING TO TELL YA...

MAKE IT SNAPPY... I DON'T WANT THIS WOOD GLUE TO SET...

LET ME GET ONE MORE LOAD INTO THE DRYER, SON...

TIME-OUT!

LISTEN...WE TRULY APPRECIATE ALL YOUR HELP, WE REALLY DO...

BUT- UM... IT'S A BIT MUCH.

YOU'VE BEEN WORKING AROUND THE HOUSE NON-STOP SINCE THE DAY WE MOVED IN!

JOEY IS ABSOLUTELY RIGHT, DOT...WE'RE SMOTHERING THEM.

WE'RE DOING TOO MUCH AND DIDN'T REALIZE IT!

NO OFFENSE!

PASS ME THAT CABLE GUIDE, WILL YA?

GOT ANY DIP FOR MY CHIPS?

I THINK THEY MISSED THE POINT.

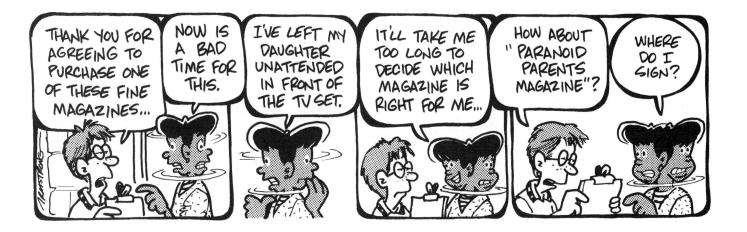

WAK!

DEXTER HIT SUNNY AT SCHOOL TODAY.

HE DID?

I THOUGHT DEXTER WAS IN LOVE WITH SUNNY!

LITTLE BOYS DON'T ALWAYS HANDLE THEIR FEELINGS APPROPRIATELY.

THAT'S NO EXCUSE.

WE HAVE TO TEACH SUNNY TO FIGHT BACK!

BIG BOYS OFTEN HAVE THE SAME PROBLEM.

I DIDN'T LIKE THE WAY YOUR PARTNER TALKED TO ME.

REALLY.

YEAH. REALLY! I THINK HE'S A RACIST!

CRUNCHY ISN'T THE LEAST BIT PREJUDICED...

HEH HEH

HE'S EQUALLY OFFENSIVE TO ALL OF OUR SUSPECTS!

THAT WOMAN HAS A PERFECT FIGURE, DOESN'T SHE, JOE?

TIME HAS FROZEN FOR A MOMENT WHILE I CONSIDER THE PROPER RESPONSE TO THAT QUESTION

I COULD SAY "YES," BUT HERE'S WHAT WOULD HAPPEN:

SO YOU'RE SAYING MY FIGURE ISN'T PERFECT! IS THAT IT?!

I COULD LIE AND SAY "NO," BUT I NEVER LIE TO MARCY! HERE'S WHY:

YOU'RE **LYING!** THE TRUST IS GONE!

THERE'S ONLY ONE OPTION HERE: I MUST NOW BECOME COMPLETELY DISORIENTED.

LOOK AT HER FIGURE, JOE! SHE'S GETTING AWAY!

MY FINGER IS IN THE WAY?☆ WHICH WAY? WHO? WHERE?

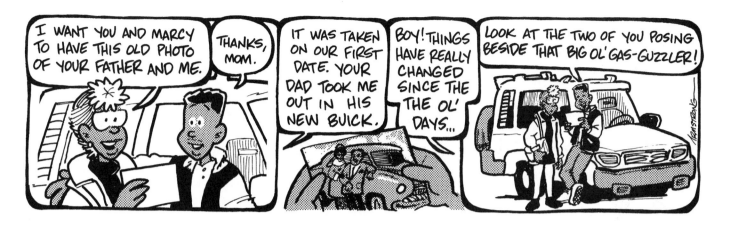

JUMPSTART

INCREDIBLE! THIS BANK HAS EVERY DOLLAR WE OWN AND NO PENS WITH INK!

YOU HAVE MY PERMISSION TO SPLURGE ON PENS!

GREAT! AS SOON AS I'M READY TO GET IN LINE, MORE PEOPLE SHOW UP!

OH, DON'T TELL ME ONE OF THE TELLERS JUST WENT TO LUNCH!

WHAT'S THAT GUY DOING... HE'S ACTUALLY CASHING IN HIS PENNIES! ON MY LUNCH BREAK!

LET'S SEE THAT MOVE AGAIN IN SLOW MOTION!

SHEESH!

WELL! IT'S ABOUT TIME! DAG!

HI, MARCY! HOW'S IT GOING, GIRL?

I CAN'T COMPLAIN...

JUMP START
BY ROBB ARMSTRONG

NEED HELP FINDING SOMETHING?

YES.

HELP ME FIND EVERYTHING ON MY LIST.

MMMM! WHAT'S THAT WONDERFUL AROMA?

CANARD AUX NAVETS.

THAT'S FRENCH FOR ROAST DUCK WITH GLAZED TURNIPS.

YOU COOKED DINNER? UNBELIEVABLE!

NOT JUST ANY DINNER, IT'S A FIVE-COURSE FRENCH MEAL WITH HOMEMADE DESSERT.

WHERE'S SUNNY?

AT MY PARENTS' HOUSE.

WHAT'S THE SPECIAL OCCASION?

BEING MARRIED TO YOU IS WHAT'S SO SPECIAL, MARCY.

HOW ROMANTIC—

Z

127

DATE DUE